Building Sandcastles

Dona Herweck Rice

✴ Smithsonian

Consultants

Brian Mandell
Program Specialist
Smithsonian Science Education Center

Amy Zoque
STEM Coordinator and Instructional Coach
Vineyard STEM School
Ontario Montclair School District

Publishing Credits

Rachelle Cracchiolo, M.S.Ed., *Publisher*
Conni Medina, M.A.Ed., *Editor in Chief*
Diana Kenney, M.A.Ed., NBCT, *Series Developer*
Emily R. Smith, M.A.Ed., *Content Director*
Véronique Bos, *Creative Director*
Robin Erickson, *Art Director*
Michelle Jovin, M.A., *Associate Editor*
Mindy Duits, *Series Designer*
Lee Aucoin, *Senior Graphic Designer*
Smithsonian Science Education Center

Image Credits: p.12 Carolyn Jenkins/Alamy; p.24 Albert Shakirov/Alamy;
all other images from iStock and/or Shutterstock.

Library of Congress Cataloging-in-Publication Data

Names: Rice, Dona, author. | Smithsonian Institution.
Title: Building sandcastles / Dona Herweck Rice.
Description: Huntington Beach, CA : Teacher Created Materials, [2020] |
   "Smithsonian." | Audience: K to grade 3. |
Identifiers: LCCN 2018049792 (print) | LCCN 2018054923 (ebook) | ISBN
   9781493868933 (eBook) | ISBN 9781493866533 (pbk.)
Subjects: LCSH: Sandcastles--Juvenile literature.
Classification: LCC TT865 (ebook) | LCC TT865 .R53 2020 (print) | DDC
   736/.96--dc23
LC record available at https://lccn.loc.gov/2018049792

Teacher Created Materials

5301 Oceanus Drive
Huntington Beach, CA 92649-1030
www.tcmpub.com
ISBN 978-1-4938-6653-3
© 2019 Teacher Created Materials, Inc.

Table of Contents

Castles of Sand

Castles are made to last. But sandcastles wash away. They are pretty enough for kings and queens. But most people would not think of living in them.

Sandcastles are works of art. And they are fun to make!

Ready to Build

You need the right tools to build sandcastles. The first tool is your mind. If you can picture a sandcastle, you can build it. Tools will help you.

This boy uses a plastic tool to build his sandcastle.

The tallest sandcastle in the world was built using many tools.

Sand

Sandcastles are made of sand, of course. First, pack the sand like mud. For this to work, the sand has to be wet. Wet sand holds together. However, if your sand is too wet, it will fall down.

A sandcastle builder packs wet sand together.

A sandcastle builder pours water onto a pile of sand.

Science & Technology

Wet Sand

Wet sand sticks because of the water. Drops of water connect the **grains** of sand. Water acts like glue that holds the grains together.

Pails

Pails are a must for great sandcastles. Press wet sand into a pail to make it hold together. You can even use a pail with a fun design. Then, flip the pail of sand into place.

This pail will give sand a fun design.

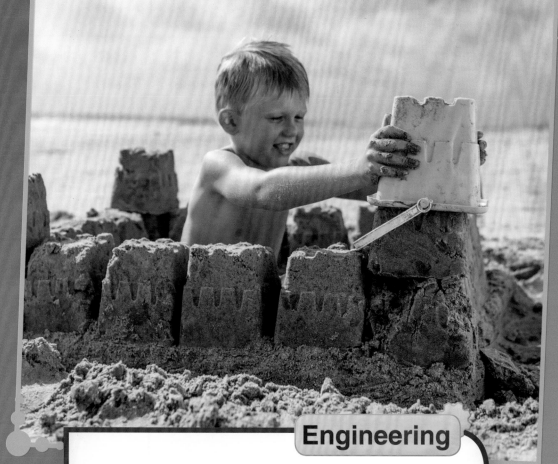

This boy uses his pail to build a sandcastle from the ground up.

Top Down

Build your sandcastle from the ground up. But **sculpt** from top to bottom. If sand falls from the top, it can ruin designs below.

Shovels

Use shovels to dig a pit for building. Then, use them to spread the ground flat. Next, use shovels to scoop sand into pails. You can also **pat** the sand into shape with them.

This girl uses a shovel to pat sand into a bucket.

Looking Good

It is important that your sandcastle has the right size and shape. This will help your castle stand strong. But how a sandcastle looks is important too. A pile of sand is not a castle!

From the Kitchen

You can use kitchen **utensils**. They will help you sculpt shapes. You can use them to make designs as well. Any kitchen tool can become a sand tool.

How do you say that?
utensils = (yoo-TEN-suhlz)

Kitchen pans can be used to sculpt sand too.

Spray Bottle

Sandcastles take time to build. Wet sand will dry in the sun and may fall apart when you touch it. Use a spray bottle of water to keep the sand wet. Keep spraying where you are working.

The sun is drying this sand.

Try, Try Again

Sandcastles can fall down. They often crack and break.

But do not give up! If your castle falls, try again. Who knows? The new design might be better than you planned!

STEAM CHALLENGE

The Problem

You have been asked to join a contest for building sandcastles! Can you make a sandcastle that is fit for a king or queen? What shape will you build?

The Goals

- Build a sandcastle that measures at least 30 centimeters (1 foot) wide by 30 centimeters (1 foot) tall.
- Build your sandcastle using sand, water, and tools for sculpting.
- Build a sandcastle that can stand for at least 15 minutes without falling.

Research and Brainstorm

Why is sand different from dirt? Can a person make a castle out of dirt? How about rocks?

Design and Build

Draw your plan. How will it work? What materials will you use? Build your model!

Test and Improve

Let your sandcastle stand for at least 15 minutes. Does it stay together? Does it crack or fall? Can you make it better? Try again.

Reflect and Share

How big do you think a sandcastle can be and still stand? How small can a sandcastle be and still be shaped and sculpted?

Glossary

grains

pat

sculpt

utensils

Career Advice
from Smithsonian

Do you want to design works of art? Here are some tips to get you started.

"Study how buildings are built. Read how to take care of buildings after they are built too." *— Sharon Park, Assistant Director of the Smithsonian's Architectural & Historic Preservation*

"Do you like solving problems creatively? Are you curious about the world? Do you like math? Then, you might enjoy being an architect." *— Michael Lawrence, Assistant Director for Exhibitions*